Options Trading Strategies

A Crash Course for Beginners to Learn How to Trade Using the Best Strategies to Maximize Profits and Reduce Risk

© Copyright 2023 by **Jeff H. Bolton**

Table of Contents

Chapter 15: How to Become a Millionaire with Options Trading 93

Conclusion 99

Introduction

Every industry has its own specialized lingo, and options trading is no exception. Let's give a quick overview that will help you understand what is being discussed when reading about options and help you navigate the markets effectively.

Ask

The price that a seller is asking for security or put another way the smallest price a seller is willing to accept to sell it.

Assignment

When the buyer of an options contract exercises their option, a notice is sent to the seller. The seller is then obligated to dispose of (in the case of a call) or purchase (in the case of a put) stocks at the strike price.

At the Money

This means that the current market price is equal to the strike price.

Bid Price

This term refers to the optimum amount that a dealer is willing to shell out for the security.

Break-Even Point

When neither a profit nor loss has been realized.

Call

The buyer of a call option has the right to buy 100 shares of a stock at the strike price at any time before the options contract expires. This is an option, so the buyer does not have to buy the shares. The seller of a call contract must buy the shares under any circumstances up to the expiration of the contract if the buyer exercises their right before the contract expires.

Commission

A fee charged by a brokerage firm to execute an option order on an exchange.

Early Exercise

If an options contract is exercised before the expiration date, it is said to be early.

Exercise

The buyer of the option exercises their right to buy stock for a call or sell the stock for a put.

Expiration Date

Options contracts expire on the third Friday of every month. When you see an option quote such as:

In the Money (Call)

This refers to the occurrence of when the current market price exceeds the strike price. This is the gross profit per share (not including premium and other fees).

In the Money (Put)

For a put contract, it is in-the-money when the current stock price is less than the strike price.

Index Options

An index option doesn't have individual stocks as the underlying. Instead, the underlying is an index like the NASDAQ. An index option can't be exercised until the expiry date.

Intrinsic Value

An apt example would be – if the current price is at $10, then the market price is at $20, the intrinsic value would be $10. If the current price were $25, the intrinsic value would be $15.

Legs

A leg is one part of a position when there are two or more options or positions in the underlying stock.

Long

Long means ownership when it is held in your account. You can belong on a stock or an option.

Margin Requirement

If you are selling options, you will be required to deposit some cash with the brokerage to cover your positions. In other words, it is cash in your account with the brokerage to buy or sell shares as required by your obligations in the options contract.

Option Chain

An option chain is something you'll look at when viewing available options online. It's basically a table for the options available for a given underlying stock. For the given expiration date, the option chain will include all puts and calls and strike prices that are available.

Out-of-the-Money

If your price $50 but the market is $40, you're "out of the money" $10. If your strike price for a put is $50, but the market price is $60, you're out of the money $10.

Put

The buyer of a put option has the right to sell 100 shares at the strike price on or before the expiry date. The seller of a put option has an obligation to buy 100 shares if required by the buyer.

Roll a Long Position

Rolling a long position means to sell options and then acquire others with the same underlying stock but with different strike prices and expiration dates.

Roll a Short Position

Rolling a short position means buying to close an existing position and selling for the purposes of opening new positions with different strike prices and expiration dates "rolled out" in time.

Series

Options are grouped together in series on the markets. Options in the same series can be calls or puts, but they have the same expiration date and strike price.

Short

Selling a security that you don't actually own.

Strike Price

It is the amount per share of the agreed-upon contract. If the option to buy or sell is exercised by the purchaser of an options contract, the shares must be bought or sold at the strike price.

When you look at options online, the strike price is given at the end of the options symbol. For example, you might see:

Time Value

How long is left until an options contract expires? Generally, more time value will mean that an option is worth more when trading. The reason is that the more time until the option expires, the more chance there is for the underlying stock to beat the strike price.

Time Decay

Time decay is simply a measure of the decrease in the time value of an options contract.

Underlying

The underlying stock is the specific stock that the option contract is based on. This is the stock that is actually traded if the option is exercised.

Weekly

A weekly is a kind of option that expires within a week, rather than a monthly time frame. Since weekly's have a short time value, they are cheaper, but the risks involved are higher. Investors who like weeklies are hoping to capitalize on an option that tightly fits a given date coming up in the near future. Weeklies usually expire on Friday afternoons at the market close. Weeklies help traders that are trying to exploit short term events for profits. For example, investors might target an earnings report or an anticipated product announcement.

Three ways to close an options contract

Now let's learn the three basic ways that you can close an options contract, now that we have some familiarity with the lingo.

- The option expires out of the money. That means that the option is worthless. You do nothing and move on. The seller of the option simply pockets the premium.
- The option expires in the money. In that case, it's up to the buyer to exercise their options. If they choose to, then the underlying stock is traded.
- The last option is to sell the option – i.e., trade it to someone else – prior to the expiration date. If you are losing money on the options contract, you can trade it and cut your losses now, rather than finding out what will happen if you hold it to the expiration date. On the other hand, if you are profiting from the option, you can sell it to get out now with profits.

Chapter 1: The Options Trader Mindset

Trading psychology is the mental state and emotions that determine the success or failure of trading options. It represents the aspect of your behavior that dictates the decisions you make when faced with a trade. The psychology is vital to any trade and can be compared to experience, knowledge, and skills in determining your success as a trader.

The Basics of Trading Psychology

We associate trading psychology to some behaviors and emotions that are often the triggers for catalysts for decisions. The most common emotions that every trader will come across are fear and greed.

Fear

At any given time, fear represents one of the worst kinds of emotions that you can have. Check in your newspaper one day, and you read about a steep selloff, and the next thing is trying to rack your brain about what to do next, even if it isn't the right action at that time.

Many investors think that they know what will happen in the next few days, which makes them have a lot of confidence in the outcome of the trade. This leads to investors getting into the trade at a level that is too high or too low, which in turn makes them react emotionally.

As the trader puts a lot of hope on the single trade, the level of fear tends to increase, and hesitation and caution kick in.

Fear is part of every trader, but skilled traders have the capacity to manage the fear. There are various types of fears that you will experience, let us look at a few of them:

The Fear to Lose

Have you ever entered a trade, and all you could think about is losing? The fear of losing makes it hard for you to execute the perfect strategy or enter or exit a strategy at the right time.

As a trader, you know that you need to make timely decisions when the strategy signals you to take one. When you have fear guiding you, the level of confidence drops, and you don't have the ability to execute the strategy the right way, at the right time. When a strategy fails, you lose trust in your abilities as well as strategy.

When you lose trust in many of the strategies, you end up with analysis paralysis, whereby you don't have the capacity to pull the trigger on any decision that you make. Making a move becomes a huge challenge.

When you cannot pull the trigger, all you can think about is staying away from the pain of losing, while you need to move towards gains.

No trader likes to lose, but it is a fact that even the best traders will make losses once in a while. The key is for them to make more profitable trades that allow them to stay in the game.

When you worry too much, you end up being distracted from your execution process, and instead, you focus on the results.

To reduce the fear of trading, you need to accept losses. The probability of losing or making a profit is 50/50, and you need to accept this fact and accept a trade, whether it is a sell or a buy signal.

The Fear of a Positive Trend Going Negative (and Vice Versa)

Many traders choose to go for quick profits and then leave the losses to run down. Many traders want to convince themselves that they have made some money for the day, so they tend to go for a quick profit so that they have the winning feeling.

So, what should you do instead? You need to stick with the trend. When you notice a trend is starting, it is good to stay with the trend until you have a signal that the trend is about to reverse. It is only then that you exit this position.

To understand this concept, you need to consider the history of the market. History is good at pointing out that times change, and trends can go either way. Remember that no one knows the exact time the trend will start or end; all you need to do is wait upon the signal.

The Fear of Missing Out

For every trade, you have people that doubt the capacity of the trade to go through. After you place the trade, you will be faced with many skeptics that will doubt the whole procedure and leave you wondering whether to exit the strategy or not.

This fear is also characterized by greed – because you aren't working on the premise of making a successful trade rather the fact that the security is rising without you having a piece of the pie.

This fear is usually based on information that there is a trend that you missed that you would have capitalized on.

This fear has a downside – you will forget about any potential risk associated with the trade and instead think that you have the capacity to make a profit because other people benefited from the action.

Fear of Being Wrong

Many traders put too much emphasis on being right that they forget that this is a business they should run the right way. They also forget that being successful is all about knowing the trend and how it affects their engagement.

When you follow the best timing strategy, you create many positive results over a certain time.

The uncanny desire to focus on always being right instead of focusing on making money is a great part of your ego, and to stay on the right path; you need to trade without your ego for once.

If you accommodate a perfectionist mentality when you get into trades, you will be after failure because you will experience a lot of losses as well. Perfectionists don't take losses the right way, and this translates into fear.

Ways to Overcome Fear in Trading

As you can see, it is obvious that fear can lead to losses. So, how can you avoid this fear and become successful?

Learn

You need to find a way to get knowledge so that you have the basis for making decisions. When you know all there is to know about options, you know what to buy and when to sell, and learn which ones to watch. You are then more comfortable making the right decisions.

Have Goals

What are your short term and long-term goals? Setting the right goals helps you to overcome fear. When you have goals, you have rules that dictate how you behave, even in times of fear. You also have a timeline for your journey.

Envision the Bigger Picture

You always need to evaluate your choices at all times and see what you have gained or lost so far for taking some steps. Understanding the mistakes you made gives you guidance to make better decisions in the future.

Start Small

Many traders that subscribe to fear have lost a lot before. They put a lot of funds on the line and ended up losing, which in turn made them fear to place other trades. Begin with small sums so that you don't risk too much to put fear in you. Once you get more confident, you can invest larger sums so that you enjoy more profit.

Use the Right Strategy
Having the right trading strategy makes it easy to execute your trades successfully. Make sure you look at various options trading strategies so that you know which one is ideal for your situation and skills. Many strategies can help you succeed, but others might leave you confused. If you have a strategy that doesn't give you the returns you desire, then adjust it to suit your needs over time. Refine it till you are comfortable with its performance.

Go Simple
When you have a strategy that is simple and straightforward, you will be less likely to lose confidence along the way because you know what to expect. Additionally, the easier the strategy, the faster it will be to spot any issues.

Don't Hesitate
At times you have to jump into the fray even if you aren't so comfortable with the way it works. Once you begin taking steps, you will learn more about the trade. However, you always need to be prepared when taking any trade. The more prepared you are, the easier it will be for you to run successful trades.

Don't Give Up
Things might not always go as you expect them to do. Remember that mistakes are there to give you lessons that will make you a better trader. When you lose, take time to identify the mistake you made and then correct it, then try again.

Chapter 2: What is Options Trading?

What Are Stock Options

To get an understanding of the meaning of stock options, we first have to know the meaning of the two words independently.

Stock refers to:

- The total money a company has from selling shares to individuals.
- A portion of the ownership of the company that can be sold to members of the public

Option (finance) refers to:

A contract that provides the buyer with the right, though not the obligation, to sell or buy an asset at an agreed-upon strike price at a specified date based on the type of option

Now that we know the meaning of both stocks and options, we can easily define stock options. We can define the term in the following ways:

Stock options provide an investor with the right to sell or buy a stock at a set price and date.

The stock option can also refer to an advantage in the form of an opportunity provided by a company to any employee to buy shares in a company at an agreed-upon fixed price or a discount.

Stock options have been a topic of interest in recent years. We are having more and more people engaging in options trading. The profitability of stock options has resulted in a lot of debates. Some say it's a scam; others claim that it is not a worthy investment, while others say that they are minting millions from it. All these speculations draw us to one question, which is what are stock options? For us to accurately answer this question, we will have to go through stock options keenly. We will be required to know all about it and what it entails. This information makes it easy to make judgments with actual facts as opposed to using assumptions. You will get to say something that you can actually back up. Having knowledge gives you an added advantage and places you in a powerful position.

Understanding Stock Options

For us to understand stock options, we consider the following:

- **Strike Price**

For one to know if a stock can be exercised, they will need to consider the strike price. By the time an option gets to the expiration date, there is a price that it is expected to have. This price should be lower or higher than the stock price, and it is what we refer to as the strike price of an underlying asset. If, as an investor, you predict that the value of the stock will increase, you can purchase a call option at the set strike price. When it comes to putting options, the strike price will be the price at which an asset is traded by the option buyer by the time the contract expires. The strike price can also be referred to as the exercise price. It is a major factor to consider while establishing the option value. Depending on when the options are carried out, the strike price will differ. As an investor, it is good to keep track of the strike price since it helps in identifying the quality of an investment.

- **Expiration date**

An expiration date refers to the period in which a contract is regarded as worthless. Stocks have expiration dates. The period between when they were purchased and the expiry date, indicate the validity of an option. As a trader, you are expected to utilize the contracts to your advantage within this time frame. You can trade as much as you can and get high returns within the period of buying and the period of expiry. Learn to utilize the time provided adequately. If you are not careful, the option may expire before you get a chance to exercise it.

Contacts

Contracts refer to the amount of shares an investor is intending to purchase. One hundred shares of an underlying asset are equal to one contract. Contracts aid in establishing the value of s stock. Contracts tend to be valuable before the expiry date. After the expiry date, a contract can be regarded as worthless. Knowing this will help you discover the best time to exercise a contract. In a case where a trader purchases ten contracts, he or she gets to 10 $ 350 calls. When the stock prices go above $ 350, at the expiry trade, the trader gets the chance to buy or sell 1000 shares of their stock at $350. This happens regardless of the stock price at that particular time. In an event whereby the stock is lower than $350, the option will expire worthlessly. This will result in making a complete loss as an investor. You will lose the whole amount you used to purchase options, and there is no way of getting it back. If you intend to invest in options trading, it is good to become aware of the contracts and how you can exercise them for a profitable options trading outcome.

Premium

The premium refers to the money used to purchase options. You can obtain the premium by multiplying the call price and the number of contracts by 100. The '100' is the number of shares per contract. This is more like the investment made by the trader expecting great returns. While investing, you will expect that the investment you chose to engage in will result in a profitable outcome. No one gets in business anticipating a loss. You find that one is always hopeful that the investment they have chosen to engage in will be beneficial. You will constantly look forward to getting the best out of a trade.

- ## Options in the Stock Market

Stock options are not as hard as people make them appear. At times people try to make them seem difficult, yet it is an easy thing that can be grasped by almost everyone. As a beginner, do not be discouraged into thinking that options trading is a difficult investment. You will be surprised how easy it is, and you will wonder why you never invested in it sooner. When engaging in stock options, there are four factors the investors will have to consider. Putting these factors into consideration will have a positive impact on their trade.

- ## The Right, But Not the Obligation

What comes in your mind when you read this statement? Well, when we talk or rights, we mean that you have the freedom to purchase a certain type of option. When we talk of obligation, we are referring to the fact that one does not have a legal authority to exercise a duty. Options do not give traders a legal authority to carry out a duty. This means that there is freedom to trade, but it is not legally mandated.

- **Buying or Selling**

As a trader, you are given the right to purchase or trade an option. There are two types of stock that one can choose from. We have the put option and the call option. Both differ and have their individual pros and cons. If you intend to trade in options, it is important that you equip yourself with adequate knowledge before trading or purchasing stocks. This information will have an impact on your expected income. The stocks you choose to buy or sell will dictate if you will earn high returns or if you will end up making a loss.

- **Set Price**

There is a certain price that has been set to exercise the option. The price will vary depending on the option type. Some stock options tend to be valued more than other options. There are a number of factors that will influence the price of options.

- **Expiry Date**

The expiry date is when a contract will be considered useless. Stock options have an expiry date. The date is set to determine the value of an option. Any period before the expiration date, a contact is regarded as being valid. This means that it can be utilized to generate income at any point before the expiry date. When it gets to the expiry date, a trader has no power to exercise the option. This is as a result of the contract being regarded as worthless. As an investor, it is good to constantly ensure that your investment is within the duration of its validity.

Chapter 3: How Options Prices are Determined

Options prices are determined in part by the price of the underlying stock. But options prices are also influenced by the time left to expiration and some other factors. We are going to go over all the different ways that the price of a given option can change and what will be behind the changes. It's important to have a firm grasp of these concepts so that you don't go into options as a naïve beginning trader.

Market price of shares

The largest factor that impacts the price of an option is the price of the investment known as the stock that is behind the option. However, it's not a 1-1 relationship. The amount of influence from the underlying stock is going to change with time. Furthermore, it depends on whether the option is in the money, at the money, or out of the money. The fraction of the options price that is due to the price of the underlying stock is called the *intrinsic value* of options.

If an option can be exactly the same as the market pricing or not be comparatively favored, it has zero intrinsic value. An option would have to be priced in the money in order to have any intrinsic value.

- For a call option, if the market price is lower than the strike price or the same, the option will have no pricing at all from the intrinsic value. If the share price is higher than the price used to trade shares via the option, the option will have intrinsic value.

- For a put option, if the share price is at or above the strike price, the option will have zero intrinsic value. If the share price is below the strike price, then the option will have some value from the stock. This is called intrinsic value.

However, to confuse matters, even when an option is at or out of the money, the price of the underlying stock has some influence that can change the value of the option. The amount of influence that the market price of the item known as the stock has on the price of the option is given by a quantity that is called *delta*. You can read the value for delta by looking at the data for any option that you are interested in trading. It is given as a decimal value ranging from 0 to 1 for call options, and it's given as a negative value for put options. The reason it's given as a negative value for put options is that this reflects the fact that if the stock price is found to increase, the price of a put option will be reduced. In contrast, if the stock price declines, the value of the put option will increase. It's an inverse relationship, and thus, the delta is negative for put options.

Implied Volatility

One of the most important characteristics of options after considering delta and time decay is the amount a stock price varies with time. Volatility will give you an idea of how wild the price swings of stock are. If you look at a stock chart, I am sure that you are used to seeing the price go up and down a lot, giving a largely jagged curve. The more that it fluctuates, and the bigger the fluctuations in price, the higher the volatility. Of course, everything is relative and so you can't say that any stock has an "absolute" level of volatility. What is done is the volatility for the entire market is calculated, and then the volatility of a stock is compared to the volatility of the market as a whole. When looking at the stocks themselves, this is given by a quantity called beta.

One of the things that make options valuable is the probability that the price of the stock will move in a direction that is favorable to the strike price. When an option goes in the money, or deeper in the money (that is the share price moves even higher relative to the strike price of a call, or lower relative to the strike price of a put), the value of the option can increase by a large margin.

If a stock is more volatile, there is more chance of this happening, since the price is going to be going through larger price swings. Therefore, the higher the implied volatility, the higher the price of the option.

Time Decay

The important thing to do is check theta every afternoon so you can estimate what the cost is going to be for holding the option overnight. Time decay is an exponential phenomenon, so it decays faster the closer you get to the expiration date. The important path for the trader is knowing when other factors are going to be more important than time decay, you are not simply going to sell off your option because it's going to lose value from time decay the following morning.

Risk-Free Rate

You are also going to see the risk free rate quoted for an option. This is the interest rate that you could earn on an ideal safe investment. Generally speaking, this would be the interest you could earn from a 10-year U.S. treasury over the time period of the option. In normal times, this is an important factor to consider. Rising interest rates (that is significantly rising) can lower the value of options. In recent years, interest rates have been very low, and changes in interest rates have been small and very conservative. So at the present time at least, this is not really something to worry about.

Summary: The Greeks

The Greeks tell us the sensitivity to changes in the factors behind the contract that impact the price of the option.

- Delta: This measures how much the price of the option will vary if there is a single dollar move in the share price, and it also gives the probability that the option contract will come to an end favorably for the buyer. That is, it would be in the money.
- Theta: This tells you the amount the price would decline if a single day has passed. Its impact is felt when the market opens.
- Vega: This measures how responsive the option is if there is an alteration in implied volatility. It tells you how much the price of the option will change in response to a 1% change in the implied volatility.
- Rho: This tells you how responsive the option is to a variation of the risk-free interest rate. It estimates how much the price of the option will change in response to a 1% change in interest rates.
- Gamma: This tells you how much delta will be varying as a result of a change in the underlying stock price.

Before you invest in an option, you should check the values of the Greeks. Then determine the relationship of the option strike price. Ask if it is in the money or out of the money, and determine what the implied volatility is.

Chapter 4: Basic Options Strategies

The Advantages of the Options Trading System

By opening a part of the position (half, for example), we avoid losing a lot of money if we make a mistake on the meaning of the market. In a way, the trader tests the market. We only strengthen our position when the market gives us the reason. In this case, we expect confirmation or a new low point (in a bull market) or high point (in a bear market) in the current trend. For example, if we are buyers, it is possible to strengthen one's position when the RSI lands on the neutrality zone. The placement of the stop will be slightly below the base, which has been broken to strengthen the position.

This technique allows the trader to avoid the classic mistake of getting out of a winning position too early and hesitating to cut a losing position. If the position results in a loss, it will not be too big, and therefore, the trader will not hesitate to cut it. Indeed, when the loss is heavy, it is often painful, and traders prefer to go into hope mode rather than face it. In addition, this approach allows the trader to play the movement in all its amplitude since it will strengthen its position, which will prevent it from going out quickly.

In addition, the trader who strictly applies his plan will avoid downward averaging. This serious fault is often fatal. From now on, with this method, the trader will strengthen his position only when the market evolves in his direction and will not cut it too fast or with a small gain. Finally, the last advantage of this method is that it allows testing the market. If the stock does not react as expected, the loss will be only 50% of the loss that would have been incurred if the entire position had been opened at the very beginning. Thus, this method allows the trader to strictly adhere to the stock market adage: "Cut your losses and ride your winners."

The Limits of the Options Trading System

This method presents the risk of strengthening a position while a market reversal is emerging. It is not effective in a market without a trend because the trader will strengthen its position on an extreme level (high point or low point). He must, therefore, be convinced that there is a tendency to apply this approach. This method adapts badly to a market without trend, but even in this case, it presents limited risks.

The Classic System: Open Its Position in One Time

The classic method is to fully open its position and then take profits during the upward movement (for a purchase) or downward movement (for a sale).

The Limits of the Classical System

This system is mainly adapted to a market without a trend. It should be noted that the losses are much greater than for the options trading system and that the performance is not necessarily greater. Nevertheless, when the market is volatile, this system is the most efficient. The trader will have to focus on carefully selecting his positions (thus increasing his probability of success) and taking profits faster.

A Pragmatic Method to Maximize Trading

One of the main attractions of technical analysis is that it does not present huge barriers to entry. It is less demanding than the fundamental analysis in terms of knowledge to acquire. Fundamental analysis generally requires long and solid academic training in economic and financial analysis. This training is usually difficult to acquire, which can discourage more than one.

The researcher Olivier Godechot conducted a sociological study on traders operating in a Paris trading room. This research found that traders and other financial operators had little control over economic reasoning. The author even goes ahead to say that the market economist was merely popularizing the economy and did not push his analyzes very far.

Moreover, even with this method of analysis, investors are not necessarily well equipped to understand the significant and persistent discrepancies in the price of a financial asset compared to its fundamental value. The tests conducted by Meese and Rogoff (1983) have shown that it is impossible for fundamental analysis to predict the evolution of exchange rates. They even go so far as to argue that a naïve model was often more efficient than a model based on fundamental analysis.

The frequent and large discrepancies between the price of a financial asset and its fundamental value (assessed by financial analysts) are hardly explained by the fundamentals, or they are posterior. Finally, the technical analysis is not reduced in the short term, as many experts say. This method offers reliability in the forecasts made, and this as well in the short term as on the medium and long term, as we will see it thereafter.

Equal Treatment for All Stakeholders

For the Orthodox school, an efficient market is characterized by the transparency of information. But many insiders (employees of a company, business bankers, family, friends, financial analysts, etc.) have some privileged information, which they can take advantage of. Everyone is not equal in the phase of information.

For the proponents of technical analysis, all the information available at a given moment is integrated into the courses. If a company intends to report poor results, it is likely that this information is visible on the price, and the technical analysis offers the opportunity to anticipate this negative news. Very often, insiders will seek to get rid of their securities, which cause a decline in stock prices (no apparent news) and are a sure sign for seasoned operators.

The role of the technical analyst is to detect the moments when a title will shift without valid reason and, therefore, to be alert all the time. The graph contains all the information investors' need, which puts them on an equal footing. Some economists even go so far as to say that technical analysis does not necessarily contradict the assumption of market efficiency since it is based on the same assumptions. This approach is attractive and reassures private investors, who have the same information as professionals.

With technical analysis, performance will be primarily a function of personal discipline and experience. Indeed, having the same information does not mean that its use will be the same for everyone. Some people will know how to exploit it better than others and will react appropriately. Implicitly, this means that using the same analysis tool does not necessarily imply consistency in decision making. The psychological dimension that explains the effectiveness of technical analysis also makes it possible to understand why individuals do not make the same decisions while basing themselves on the same information.

Chapter 5: Option Prices and Valuation

At-The-Money (ATM)

Before we get to that, let's check some important market jargon. The first term we need to know is called "At-The-Money." Calls are easier for people to understand because if you are not experienced as an in-depth market trader, you are not used to thinking in terms of shorting stocks. Normal people want stock prices to rise. As you learn more about options trading, you will find out that it is not always the best thing. But calls have an intrinsic appeal to that natural belief, thought process, and desire.

A call option *is* called at-the-money when the price in the market of a certain stock is above the average strike price of the option. So, if you have an option with a strike price of $75 and the stock is trading at $80 a share, it is at-the-money. In short, at-the-money call options are worth a lot more than options that are not at-the-money. We can take a look at the options calculator to see what the differences can be.

So, I have set up a hypothetical stock which is trading at $80 dollars a share. We will consider an option that expires in 14 days. Just for the record, the implied volatility is 16%, and the risk-free rate is 0.3% (we will explain what that means in a minute).

Setting the strike price at $75, we find that the option (in this case, a call) is priced at $5.03. Once again, remember that it is for a single share; the total price of the option would be $503.

Now let's consider another option with all the same characteristics but say that this one has a strike price of $70. The price of this option is $10.01, or $1001 to buy the option. The option with the strike price of $70 is also at-the-money, but it's more at-the-money then the option with the strike price of $75.

Another way to express this concept is by saying that it is deeper at-the-money.

If the share price is exactly equal to the strike price, the option is said to be at the money. The odds of an option being exactly at the money in the real world are slim, but they can be very close to the money. These types of options can be of interest because, if the stock price goes beyond the strike, the value of the option can suddenly increase by a large margin.

For a call option, the probability of the share price moving above the strike price can actually be fairly high. Using the example of a strike price at $75, the price of the option would be $0.92 (you would have to pay $92 to purchase the option). If the share price rises to $76 later that afternoon, the price of that call will jump to $1.53.

This kind of price change illustrates why people find trading options so appealing. If you sold right then, that would net you $61 in profit for each option contract.

Out-of-The-Money (OTM)

When the strike price is higher than the share price on the market, we say that the option is out of the money.

Options don't need to be at-the-money in order to make a profit. Depending on the direction of price movement, you can earn profits from out of the money options as well. We can illustrate this with call options.

If the stock price is rising, the prices of out of the money calls are going to rise as well. So, we shall set up a similar scenario where there are 14 days until option expiration, but, this time, assume that the strike price is $77. Suppose the share price is $75, which is lower than the strike; the option is out of the money.

If the share price rises over the next couple of days, you can actually make a decent profit. The good thing about out of the money options is they are relatively cheap.

Using our example, the $77 strike would cost $0.27 ($27 to buy).

Now let's suppose that, two days later, the share price rises to $76.50. The option is still out of the money. However, the price of the option will rise because the share price is rising. It turns out that under these conditions, the price of the option would be $0.66 at that point. That means you could turn around and sell it for $66 when you had purchased it two days earlier for $27.

Many experts don't recommend trading out of the money options. But they remain a great alternative for people that don't have much money to start making profits. This can work if there is a large price move for the underlying stock, and you only hold the option for a couple of days. If there is a lot of movement within a single day, you can actually make substantial profits.

Let's consider a real option for Apple. Consider one with the strike price of $220 that expires in 16 days. At the market opening, Apple was $192.50 a share. At that time, the call option was priced at $0.08: you could have purchased each option contract for a mere $8. Later in the morning, the share price of Apple rose to $195.76. That drove the price of the $200 strike price option to $0.16 (or for all 100 shares, $16). So, we would have an opportunity to double our money, and to make it significant; you could buy multiple options simultaneously. Remember to always check the liquidity. Looking at the volume, it is 102 for that option, and the open interest is 269. That would be enough liquidity to close the position in a timely fashion.

One thing to remember about options is that if an option expires and it is out of the money, it is also worthless (it "expires worthless"). This holds true for the money options as well. If the option is at-the-money at expiration, the price of the option is (share price – the strike price).

Chapter 6: Types and Styles of Options

There is a wide range of types and styles of options accessible. This segment gives a picture of each kind just as some essential wording each option investors ought to be comfortable with.

Call Options

A call option gives the investor the right (not the commitment) to buy the fundamental stock, security, item, or other instruments, at a particular cost within the time of the contract. The predefined cost is known as the strike cost. A speculator who is bullish on the stock, which means he anticipates that the stock should go up within a short time or inside the particular time span, would buy a call option.

For instance, say Investor A thinks stock XYZ is going to post high income one month from now, and the stock will go higher. So she buys a call option on the stock for $20. The option agreement determines that she can buy 100 portions of XYZ at a strike cost of $100 inside the following 60 days. If the cost of the stock falls beneath $100, then she won't practice the option. The agreement will terminate uselessly, and she will have lost the $20 price tag. In any case, if the cost of the stock transcends $100, state to $130, then she will practice the option, buy the stock for $100, and afterward, sell it at the higher market cost. She has now made a pleasant benefit.

Put Options

A put option is something contrary to a call option. It gives the owner the right (however not the commitment) to sell the fundamental stock at a predetermined value (the strike cost) inside the predefined time span. An investor who is bearish on the stock, which means he thinks the stock cost is going down, would buy a put option.

For instance, say Investor B thinks stock XYZ is overrated and will decrease in cost throughout the following 60 days. He buys a put option on the stock for $20. The agreement gives him the option to sell the stock for $120 inside the following 60 days. If the stock transcends $120 per share, then he would not practice the option. It would lapse useless, and he has lost his underlying speculation. If rather the cost of the stock dips under $120, to state $90, then he would practice his entitlement to sell the offers at $120 and pocket the distinction as a profit.

Using Call and Put Options to Make a Profit

There are various ways you can use call and put options. For instance, assume you believe that portions of US banks that are as of now selling for $200 per share are undervalued and will go higher in the following couple of months. You need more money to buy at least 100 portions of stock, yet might, in any case, want to bring in money from the ascent in the stock. For this situation, you could buy a call option on the stock, which would cost just a small amount of the cost of the stock. So you buy the call option, and you presently reserve the option to buy 100 portions of the stock at $200 whenever in the following 60 days.

You may be thinking, how am I going to buy the stock in the next 60 days for $200 per share if I don't have the money? The appropriate response is that you don't really need to buy the stock to make a profit. If your impulses are right and the stock cost rises above $200, then your call option will turn out to be increasingly important. At the end of the day, as the stock value rises, the value of your option agreement likewise rises. You will have the option to sell the option agreement itself, rather than the stock, and make a benefit. The higher the value rises, the more your agreement will be worth.

This works a similar route for a put option, but in this situation, you need the stock cost to fall. As the cost of the hidden security drops, the value of your put option will rise. The further the value falls, the more important is your option.

As should be obvious, by buying options, you can make a profit whether or not the stock is going up or down in cost.

Styles of Options

The past segments have given a check of the two essential sorts of options, calls and puts. This segment will assist you in understanding the different styles of options accessible.

Most options that you will buy will can be categorized as one of two classifications, American or European. These are once in a while known as vanilla options. The principle distinction between the two is the point at which you can practice the option.

<u>American Options</u>

American options can be practiced whenever before the expiry date. Most options on stocks and value are of this sort. These are additionally the kind of agreements exchanged on fates trades.

European Options

European options must be practiced on the lapse date characterized in the agreement. These sorts of options are, for the most part, exchanged over-the-counter (OTC) advertise.

The values of the two option styles are determined marginally distinctively, and their termination dates are additionally unique. American options lapse the third Saturday of the month, while European options terminate the Friday before the third Saturday of the month.

Similitudes between the two incorporate the result and the strike cost. The result, either for calls or puts, is determined similarly for the two kinds. In like manner, the strike costs ordinarily are the equivalent.

Barrier Options

Barrier options are not the same as different sorts talked about so far in that all together for the option to result in the cost of the basic security must cross a specific level. They can be either be put or call options. There are four sorts of barrier options, which are plot beneath:

*Down-and-Out Barrier Options: A Down-and-Out Barrier Option gives the holder the privilege however not the commitment to buy (on account of a call) or sell (on account of a put) portions of a hidden resource at a foreordained strike cost since the cost of that advantage didn't go beneath a foreordained barrier during the option lifetime. That is, when the cost of the hidden resource falls underneath the barrier, the option is "took out" and no longer conveys any worth. Henceforth the name out for the count.

*Down-and-In Barrier Options: A down-and-in option is something contrary to a done for barrier option. Down-and-in options possibly convey value if the cost of the fundamental resource falls beneath the barrier during the options lifetime. If the barrier is crossed, the holder of the down-and-in option has the option to buy (if it is a call) or sell (if it is a put) portions of the hidden resource at the foreordained strike cost on the termination date.

*Up-and-Out Barrier Options: An up-and-out barrier option is like a done for barrier option, the main contrast being the arrangement of the barrier. Instead of being taken out by falling beneath the barrier cost, up-and-out options are taken out if the cost of the hidden resource transcends the foreordained barrier.

*Up-and-In Barrier Options: An up-and-in barrier option is like a down-and-in option; anyway, the barrier is set over the present cost of the hidden resource, and the option might be substantial if the cost of the basic resource arrives at the barrier before lapse.

Chapter 7: Call Spreads Strategy

Bull Call Spread Strategy

The bull call spread assumes that you have a bullish view on the market based on your technical analysis. The beauty of this strategy is that it can be adjusted, just like a collar, but without the need for establishing a long stock position. Indeed, all spread strategies have this inherent advantage to them.

This strategy works best in markets that are titled bullish but not explicitly so. What I mean is that often the market heads in a particular direction, but you'll find that it meanders about, diving as often as it rises with a small net push upwards. This sort of see-saw movement is perfect for the bull call spread.

Execution

The bull call spread has two legs to it:

1. A long at or in the money call
2. A short out of the money call

The primary profit generator in this strategy is the long call. This is what captures the upward movement of the stock and enables you to earn the increased premium via the increased intrinsic value of the option. The short call is effectively your profit target, or slightly beyond it and increases your overall profit, and you earn income from the premium upon writing it.

Let's look at how the math works out using good old AMZN. Our market price is still \$1833.51, so to establish the first leg of this trade, let's choose an in the money or at the money option, from the near month contracts. The closest we can get is 1835, which is being offered at $63.65 per share.

Next, what would be an appropriate target price? Well, this depends on how you read the market. If it is ranging sideways, but with a slightly bullish title, placing your target at the range boundary is a good idea. Obviously, your short call will need to be beyond this limit. Let's say our target is $1862. This makes writing the 1865 strike call an attractive option. The premium we will receive on writing the option is $44.55 per share.

So how does the math work out?

Cost of trade entry = Cost of long call - Premium from short call = 63.65-44.55 = $19.10 per share.

Maximum gain = Short call strike price - long call strike price = 1865-1835 = $30 per share.

Maximum loss = cost of trade entry.

Your trade entry equals the maximum possible loss because if the price of the stock decreases, as a worst-case scenario, your long call expires worthless and you get to keep the full premium from the short call. Your maximum profit is capped by the strike price of the short call.

Note that you need not be worried about the short call moving into the money. This is because you have the lower long call covering this position. In such a scenario, you simply exercise the lower call and use that to fulfill the higher call's exercise. The reward to risk ratio of this particular example is pretty decent if not amazing.

Remember that this strategy takes advantage of sluggish markets or non-committal markets with a slight bullish tilt to them. In such markets, a directional trader stands a very high chance of being wiped out. Viewed in this light, the advantage of this strategy is obvious.

Bear Call Spread Strategy

Just like the bull call spread takes advantage of sluggish bull markets, strategy takes advantage of sluggish bear markets. The best time to put both of these strategies into action is towards the end of trends where counter trend participation is getting higher by the minute. The market is about to move into an accumulative or distributive phase in preparation for a trend change.

Execution

The bear call spread contains two legs within it:

1. An at the money or near the money short call
2. An out of the money long call

The primary instrument of profit is the short call, which takes advantage of the price decreasing while the long call caps the downside. The primary earning factor in this trade is the premium you will earn on writing the short call. Similar to the bull call, your maximum profit and loss are capped, and this gives you a great view of your trade's probabilities right off the bat.

Let's look at how this would work with the current levels of AMZN. With a market price of $1833.50, the closest at the money call in the far month is the 1835 strike call. Writing this earns us a premium of $60.15 per share (the bid price of the contract). When it comes to deciding the strike price of the long call, you want to place this beyond the closest relevant resistance level.

Let's say this happens to be the 1840 level. The premium for this happens to be $58.10 per share.

So, let's look at how the math will work out:

Cost of trade entry = Cost of long call - Premium earned from short call = 58.1-60.15 = -$2.05 (you earn this amount on entry)

Maximum loss = Strike price of long call - Strike price of short call = 1840- 1835 = $5 per share.

Maximum gain = cost of trade entry.

The maximum gain you can earn on this trade is from the premium of the short call. However, your long call will decrease in price simultaneously so that they will offset one another. As you can see, the reward/risk profile is skewed for this strategy, with the risk being greater than the reward.

So why should you pursue this? Well, first of all, you must understand that the success rate of this strategy depends a lot on how well you can read market conditions. If the market is strongly bearish, you're better off buying a put instead of using the bear call spread. Again, it is the fact that you can produce profits in sluggish markets that makes it so attractive.

Most directional trades get wiped out in the sideways market or stay out entirely because if the market doesn't go anywhere, how can they make money. This is not the case with options, so an inverted reward to risk profile is a small price to pay. As always, your risk management is paramount, and you should work out your numbers well in advance.

Calendar Call Spread (Straddle)

To set up a straddle, you buy a put option and a call option simultaneously (buy = take a long position). The maximum loss that you can incur is the sum of the cost to buy the call option plus the sum of the cost to buy the put option. This loss is incurred when you enter the trade.

With a straddle, you buy a call option and a put option together. And they would be with the same strike price. By necessity, this means that one option is going to be in the money, and one option is going to be out of the money. When approaching an earnings call, the prices can be kind of steep, because you want to price them close to the current share price. That way, it gives us some room to profit either way the stock price moves.

A maximum loss is only incurred if you hold the position to expiration. You can always choose to sell it early if it looks like it's not going to work out and take a loss that is less than the maximum.

There is a total premium paid for entering into the position. This is the amount of cash paid for buying the call added to the money paid for buying the put. This is called the total premium. There are two breakeven points:

- To the upside, the breakeven point is the strike price + total premium paid.
- On the downside, the breakeven point is the strike price – total premium paid.

If the price of the stock moves up past the breakeven point, the put is worthless. However, the call option would earn substantial profits. On the other hand, if the stock price moved down past the lower price point, that would be the breakeven, the call option would be worthless, and the put option would earn substantial profits.

Chapter 8: Put Spreads Strategy

Bull Put Spread

Bull Put Spread is a vertical spread strategy where the investor sells a put option at a higher strike price, indicated in point B, and buys a put option with a lower strike price, point A, during the same month of fall. The investor receives a premium or credit because the higher strike price will be more valuable than the lower strike price.

Bullish sales and long-term sales spread

The investor uses this strategy if they believe the market will make stable or trade higher. The lower position option is used as hedging in case the market is trading lower, so that the investor can limit his maximum loss.

Shadow of profitability

The breakeven point for a bullish selling differential is the highest strike price minus the first receipt.

Breakeven = short put strike − premium received

Example

A spread of 70-75 bulls worth $ 2 would consist of selling a put in 75 strikes and buying a put in 70 strikes. Here, the $ 2 deposit would represent the maximum profit if the stock held above the 75-move price. Have an exercise width of $ 5 (70-75), which represents the maximum loss if the trade ends below the two exercise prices, less the first receipt to enter the transaction, in our example $ 2, leaving the investor with a maximum loss of $ 3.

The decay time works for the investor if the sales margin runs out of money because he wants the trade to run out, which allows him to keep the first down payment. Time will pass against the investor if the vertical makes the two strikes in money because they want this exchange to continue, which will give them more time for the stock to rise in price.

This is a great strategy to use if the investor feels that a stock will increase, but is not sure of its timing or wants to buffer it if the market moves sideways or depreciates slightly.

Bear Put Spread

A bearish spread is a vertical spread that is composed of both the highest long strike price and the shortest strike price, both maturing in the same month. The strike price of the strike, represented by point A, is lower than the long-selling strike, point B, which means that this strategy will always force the investor to pay for the trade. The main purpose of short selling is to help you pay the initial cost of long selling.

Breakeven

The point of discovery for a disadvantaged selling differential is the higher strike price minus the trade cost.

Balance = long-term strike - debt paid

Example

A 40-50 playback option set at $ 2.50 would consist of buying a call at 50 strikes and selling a call at 40 strikes, with a street width of $ 10 (50-40), which is the maximum that the Investors could earn in the transaction minus the premium paid to enter the transaction, in our example $ 2.50, leaving the investor with a maximum profit of $ 7.50.

The decrease in time goes against the investor if this sales gap is spent with money because they need more time for this trade to be profitable. Time would work for the investor if the vertical has the two outflows of money because they would like this operation to end, so there is more time for him to move against it.

The recommendation is not a strategy that needs to be executed very often if there is no evidence of predicted growth. Without it, there is a lower probability of successful trading that depends on the lower traded shares before the expiration date. It takes less capital to participate than just to buy stocks, which means less risk, but is still considered a lower probability of trading success.

Calendar Put Spreads

Long Put Option Strategy

The long-term options trading strategy gives the individual the right to sell an underlying part at the specified price, point A, as shown in the chart. When the investor buys a put option, he bets that the shares will fall below the strike price before the expiration date. Using a put option instead of shorting the stock reduces the risk for the investor because he can only lose the cost of the put option against an unlimited risk associated with a short of the stock.

Long Put Option

If the security increases, the long-term option will fall unnecessary, and the investor will lose only the cost of the option. Graphically speaking, a trader who sells short will have to lose more and more as stocks continue to grow. When buying a put option, especially in the short term, investors should be careful. If an investor buys multiple contracts of sale, his risk increases as well. In fact, options cannot expire without value, and so the investor loses the entire investment.

When buying put options

There are many reasons to buy put options, which can be spectacular, which means that the investor believes that the stock price will drop. A broad position option can also be used to protect against actions already taken, to protect an asset in the event of a sharp reversal of value, also called a protective position option.

Here, if the shares that were already held were immediately abandoned, the possibility of an option could increase in value, compensating for the losses incurred by the shares.

Short Put Option Strategy

With the short option strategy, the investor bets that the stock will either increase or remain stable until the option expires. If the put option expires without value, out of the money (above the strike price), the trader is left with the first premium, representing his maximum profit on the trade. In the sole option of trading, selling a put option is one of the two strategies of the bull market, and the other is the long-term call option.

The seller of the short sale is obliged to buy the shares, plus about 100 shares per contract, at strike price A if the buyer wants to exercise the contract.

Selling a position option can be valuable for investors because it allows them to increase their income, taking advantage of other traders who bet that the stock would fall. Therefore, when the short-selling strategy is used, the investor receives the former, protecting himself from a flat market with little movement. However, investors will sell their options because they are ready to buy the shares if the stock falls below the strike price at expiration.

Chapter 9: Brokers

In order to trade options, you will need to have a personal brokerage account. We will cover some of the different brokerages that are available and issues that you need to consider when making your selection.

What is a Broker

A broker is a "middleman." Although there are actual trading floors for options, just like there are stock exchanges, you don't actually call in your trading orders directly to the exchange. Instead, a broker does that on your behalf. A broker will provide several things for you, and different brokers provide different levels of support.

At the core, a broker is going to provide you with an account. This is like a bank account of sorts, but it's devoted strictly to trading. Options trading is not separate from stock trading, so you will open a brokerage account that will be used to fund trades of both stocks and options, should you decide to invest in both. A brokerage account will be connected to a personal banking account that you provide so that you will connect a bank checking account to the brokerage account. This will be used to transfer funds in and out. So, when you want to buy options, you will need to transfer money into your brokerage account. When you sell options to get money, you may have to wait several days before being able to transfer that money into your bank account. Please check with the broker you select for details.

Like bank accounts, there is a certain amount of government protection for the funds in a brokerage account, should the brokerage go under. This is provided by the Securities Investor

Protection Corporation, which insures up to \$250,000 cash in your account. Your ownership of actual securities exists outside the brokerage, and if a brokerage were to close, your account would be transferred to a new brokerage along with any securities, including options that you actively own.

Besides an account, the brokerage will place options trades on your behalf. In order to do this, they will have some kind of interface that allows you to execute your trades. In the old days, this was taken care of with a phone call to the broker or even a personal visit. Today, trades are automatically managed using a software interface. All brokers have a website that can be used to execute trades and move money between the brokerage account and your bank account. Most brokers also have mobile applications. These are fully featured and will allow you to trade stock and options and manage your account on your iPhone, iPad, or Android device. In fact, some brokers are primarily mobile-based today, but you can choose the type of interface that you prefer.

Choosing a Broker

There are many different brokers to choose from, and there are many factors that will influence the selection of a broker. The first factor to consider is the interface that the broker uses for trading. You might want to get on YouTube to look for videos posted for different brokerages to see what their trading interface looks like. Some have been designed to be extremely user friendly on mobile, such as Robinhood. However, that may come at a cost.

That cost is on the information side of the system. One of the factors to consider when opening a brokerage account is what tools they provide that can help you manage your trades. In particular, you will be looking for a trading system that will help you get the most information about trade as possible. Two systems that options traders prefer for this purpose are "Think or Swim" which is run by TD Ameritrade and Tasty Works. These systems were designed by professional options traders to facilitate the trading of options, and so they will contain a lot of the information you will need in order to get a good handle on the potential profitability of a trade, and look at things such as how the expiration date will impact a given trade.

Some readers will find the interfaces provided by these platforms to be too complex, and they might prefer the simplicity of Robinhood. Indeed, many beginning traders are gravitating to Robinhood primarily because of its simplicity and ease of use. The Robinhood platform makes it very easy to find options and execute trades, and it also has many setup trades for you to consider and execute with one tap on your smartphone.

Another factor that will be important to some traders is how long a company has been in business and its reputation. If this is important for you, then you can consider a more traditional broker like Charles Schwab or Fidelity. E-Trade, which is not nearly as old as those two companies, has been around for several decades, and it has a good reputation among traders as well.

It is important not to sweat your choice of broker too much. If you are attracted to the simple interface of Robinhood, you can actually use other tools in order to do your research. In fact, there are many free tools that can be found on the internet that include using stock charts and calculators that will estimate options values at different dates based on changing stock prices. You can even download fairly accurate calculators for options that are built in Excel spreadsheets. So, while the complete platforms of Think or Swim and Tasty Works suit many traders, you can get a great deal of the information they provide from other sources.

Other things to consider include the amount of support and even advice that is available at the broker. If you are looking for financial advice from a professional, you might be drawn toward a full service broker like Charles Schwab.

Trading Commissions

When I first got into this business, commissions were a big issue to consider. A commission is a fee charged by the broker each time you place a trade. Commissions need to be considered in order to determine whether a trade is profitable or not, and although commissions are not very large in an absolute dollar amount, it can have a major impact in many scenarios.

The good news is that commissions are rapidly disappearing from the industry. In fact, zero commission's options trading was one of the first selling points that was promoted by Robinhood when it came on the scene a few years ago, and this selling point helped to elevate its popularity. This also put competitive pressure on many of the older brokers in the industry.

As a result, many have decided to take the zero commission's route. In fact, Charles Schwab recently introduced zero commissions trading. So, the choices available to traders who are looking for a zero commission's brokerage have massively expanded just in the past year alone. While this used to be a major selling point for Robinhood, that isn't necessarily the case today. But be sure to check with brokers you are interested in to find out the details of their policy with respect to commissions.

Brokers used to rely on commissions as a major source of revenue, so some readers are probably wondering what they are doing now in order to make money. Most brokers offer enhanced services for a fee, and this is one way that they make the income they used to make from charging commissions. For example, Robinhood offers a "gold" service with more features for a small monthly fee. Large and established brokers like Schwab may offer professional financial advice to those who are willing to pay for it.

Chapter 10:   Risk management

We've now arrived at the most important things, which will ensure your trading success: managing risk and having the right mindset to ensure success. Options are an excellent choice for trading precisely because of their ability to manage risk better. This is why professional traders choose to operate with them in more complex strategies.

We'll dive into the basics of risk management and then look at the beliefs you need to possess in order to be successful in the markets.

Quantitative and Qualitative

Risk management is both qualitative and quantitative. The quantitative bit is far easier to understand since it is just a matter of crunching numbers and monitoring a bunch of statistics with regards to your account. Now, if you were trading directionally, the number of metrics you need to monitor is quite a lot.

Thankfully, when it comes to options, you only need to track a few. Let's take a look at these.

Risk Per Trade

More than anything else, it is your risk per trade that determines your success. The common wisdom is not to risk more than two percent of your capital per trade, and in the case of options trading, this is correct. Directional trading requires you to risk far less than this in order to be successful.

The true measure of a good trader is how consistent they are in risking the same percentage of their account on each and every trade. A lot of beginners get on a winning streak at times and then start playing loose with this only to be hit by a big loss that wipes out all their prior gains.

There is a school of thought that proposes that risking a fixed amount per trade, as opposed to a fixed percent, is a better model. Suffice to say that, risking the same amount will bring you greater gains per trade and exaggerate your winning streaks but will do the same to your losses.

What's more, thanks to your losses being exaggerated, you'll have to keep making more and more gains to simply breakeven constantly and this will wipe out your account pretty soon since the basic math of all this is against you. Remember, you can't predict the outcome of most trades in advance with precision. Thus, it's best to risk the same percentage of your account every trade.

Win Percent

The win percentage of your strategy, that is, the number of times you make money is one half of an important measure that determines whether you'll make money or not. Usually, thanks to the way we've been brought up and have had UR performances measured in school, we chase the highest win percentages, thinking ninety percent is better than forty.

Well, in academia, this is true. However, in the chaotic world of the markets, this is far from the case. Making money on a trade is not about being right. You can be right about the markets and still lose money in the long run. This is best explained after we look at the second half of the equation.

Average Win Percent

Your average win percent is the amount of money you win on average when you do make money, expressed as a percentage of your account, or as a multiple of the amount you risk per trade on average. So, if you risk R per trade, which might be 2% of your account, and if you make 4% on a win on average, you will make 2R per win.

The average win percent and the win percent together determine whether you'll make money or not. So out of ten trades, if you win two, a win rate of twenty percent, and your average win is 2R, you will not make money. This is because your eight losses will cost you -8R, and your wins will only amount to 4R. This is a net loss of -4R.

However, if you make 5R on average per win, you will make money with a twenty percent win rate. In this case, your losses will add up to -8R, but your wins will add up to 10R, giving you an overall profit of 2R. If you risk two percent of your account, this is a profit of 4% over ten trades.

Now, if you manage to take two hundred trades over the course of a year, you'll be making 80% in a year. This is precisely what professional traders do make, and it takes an extraordinarily high level of skill to hit such numbers. My point is that your profitability is determined by both numbers, not just a single one.

As you can see, it is perfectly possible to make money by being 'right' just twenty percent of the time. In a regular academic examination, this will guarantee your failure, but in the markets, it's just one half of an equation.

Qualitative Risk

Let's say you settle down in front of your television on the weekend and switch on the TV to catch your favorite game. You're fully prepped and have your TV and assorted accessories set just so. Your friends have come over as well and all in all, it's a great atmosphere. There's just one problem: your team's star athlete, the one on whom the result of the game hinges has turned up to the game hungover.

Now, it isn't unheard of such things to happen in pro sports, but when it does happen, you can imagine the reaction that follows. The athlete is roundly criticized as a buffoon, rightly so, and the sports media have a field day debating where he's about to be traded to next. We instinctively understand that preparation is the key to success, and turning up hungover is hardly good preparation.

Yet, how many of us sit down to trade after having just walked in from work? We're tired and frustrated from whatever is going on in that world and think we can simply waltz in and make money in the markets. The very same markets that are full of professionals who make a living from it and are responsible for the management of many millions and billions.

Do you seriously think anyone can be successful trading this way? Do you think trading is simply a matter of learning the right strategies and then implementing it with the snap of a finger? If so, this is an indicator that your mindset is incorrect and that you don't understand what trading risk management involves.

Make no mistake. You will need to prepare and have your wits fully about you as you sit down to trade. You cannot afford any distractions like checking your smartphone or try to wing something at the last minute. You need good sleep and need to exercise and eat well.

This is why I called the adrenaline-filled, coked-out atmosphere of trading floors in movies unrealistic because it is impossible to trade this way. A lot of beginners get seduced by this devil may care type of depiction and try to do the same when it comes to their own hard-earned money. Needless to say, this results in a quick wipeout, and the ones who will take their money are the traders who have prepared themselves.

You need to follow a specific mental and physical routine prior to operating in the markets. Meditation and other mental calming techniques are a great idea and will enable you to see things clearly, as they are. Also, avoid trading when things are not going well for you with your regular life.

There's no rule that says you have to trade each and every day of the year. Take adequate time to reflect on your skills and practice them well. Practice them so well that you know them by heart. The live market is not a place for you to be questioning whether the signal is valid or not. You simply need to pull the trigger and execute it.

Chapter 11:   Rolling out options

The process of rolling out describes an expiring option being replaced with an identical option. Rolling out is a great strategy to manage a losing or a winning position. This management is facilitated by closing one option position, then opening another option with a similar position with the same associated asset but varied terms.

Most times, traders use this strategy to adjust the strike price and the length of time the trader would like to hold a short or long position. This strategy is one that even a beginner needs to be aware of because any options trader who trades for an extended amount of time will encounter it at some point or the other. Rolling can be done in 3 ways. These ways are: Rolling up, Rolling down, and Rolling forward. We will look at each rolling over the type below.

Rolling Up

This method of rolling up involves closing one existing option position while opening a similar position with a higher strike price at the same time. The higher strike price is the reason for the name. This method is simple and can be done in both a short and a long position. In a short position, all the trader has to do is buy to close the existing position. In the long position, the trader needs to sell to close the existing position. The following step is opening a new position with the same associated asset and a higher strike price. From a short position, the trader needs to sell to a new position. From a long position, the trader needs to buy a new position.

The procedure remains the same regardless of whether it revolves around a put or a call option. The result is different though for put and call options. If the trader rolls up a put option, the contract becomes more expensive, thus the need for a higher strike price. If the trader rolls up a call option, the contract becomes less expensive. Therefore, the higher the strike price for a rolled up call option, the less expensive it becomes.

The effect is also affected by whether or not the put or call option is long or short. Rolling up a long put position entails selling cheaper options to make up the existing position so that the buying of more expensive options can be facilitated. On the other hand, rolling up short positions entails closing that position by buying cheaper options than writing up more expensive options.

Rolling up options is a useful strategy indeed. However, it does come with its own unique set of risks. Those risks become particularly high in volatile markets or in markets that are moving quickly in one particular direction. The changes in strike price between closing one position and entering another position can be detrimental if market value fluctuates at a high level.

There is another risk that goes by the name of slippage. Slippage is the circumstance that results when there is a time delay between two related options. This results in a price change during that time. This is a problem that many options traders face when they engage in multiple transactions that relate to one overall position. This is a problem that is particularly experienced when traders employ the use of spreads to gain multiple positions. This can be quite complex if the options trader is involved in several transactions at the same time.

Experienced traders become apt at handling this, though. To turn this problem around, the trader needs to roll up a specific transaction to close the existing position while opening up a new one at a higher strike price at the same time. Due to the complexity of this type of strategy, this is not something that is recommended for a beginner to try.

Rolling Down

Rolling down is the method that involves closing one existing position while opening a similar position with a lower strike price at the same time. It is the opposite of rolling up. It can be applied to both puts and calls, and both short and long positions. The reasons for using this method typically revolves around the trader's current circumstance and the position that he or she is in.

The first reason that he or she might use rolling down is to prevent exercising on a short put position so that the obligation of having to buy the associated asset is avoided. The trader might use rolling down to minimize losses on calls while still maintaining speculation on the associated asset recovering its value. Even though the expiration date may approach, the trader may maintain the belief that the price of the associated asset will increase again and, therefore, use rolling down to buy a call at a lower strike price. This provides impact protection and betters chances of getting a profit if the associated asset does indeed climb in value as speculated.

Lastly, rolling down is a consideration for many options traders because they would like to make a profit off-put options while still holding a position whereby they can speculate that there will be further downward movement of the associated asset value. In this situation, the trader rolls down so that he or she can purchase puts with lower strike prices to benefit further from the fall in the associated asset's value. This allows for continued profit without risking the profit that has already been made.

Rolling Forward

There are many options that an options trader can exercise when open positions are approaching the expiration date if the maximum profit is not yet realized but is still probable, and one of those options is rolling forward. Rolling forward involves moving an open position to a different expiration date so that the length of the contract is extended. In essence, this is closing an existing position and opening a corresponding position based on the same option characteristics with a different expiration date. This is also known as rolling over.

This can be done by closing the existing position and entering a new one or entering a new position and then closing the existing one. As you can see, these as separate transactions, and as such, this is a form of a legging.

There are 2 common reasons why rolling forward is used by options traders. The first reason is that the trader may have taken a certain position expecting to profit in a greater way in the short-term but realizes after that a bigger profit will be realized over a longer period. The extension of the expiration date enables the trader to continue to profit from the option.

The second reason is that the trader may have entered into a position expecting the associated acid to move in a particular direction within a certain amount of time and advanced realized that this will take longer than expected. Extending the length of the contract allows the trader to profit from the contract.

The Benefits of Rolling Out

Commission fees are lower because rolling out is conducted on one transaction rather than multiple.

Rolling out allows the trader to save and, thus, keeps more money in the pocket.

The risk of slippage is reduced because the closing and opening of options positions are done simultaneously and not as separate transactions.

Rolling over is a relatively simple strategy compared to other options trading strategies.

Chapter 12: Getting Started and Making Immediate Money With Options Trading

To trade in the options contract, you will need a derivative trading account. A derivative trading account opening is a little different from the normal stock trading account. A bit higher level of understanding is required for dealing in options as too many variables are involved.

In the trading account opening process, the broker may like to know things like:

- Your investment abilities
- Trading experience
- Understanding of the risk involved
- Investment objectives
- Number of trades you expect to do in a year and the amount of capital you would like to begin with
- Your financial profile
- Details like annual income, employment information, net worth, etc.
- Kind of derivatives you are interested in

This will help the broker in building your risk profile and would be able to allow you to trade in certain segments. It is very important to understand that you may not be allowed to trade all kinds of derivatives as some are more complicated and riskier than others.

The brokers generally categorize the traders into four levels and allow them to trade in derivative securities as per their levels. This is a good thing as it is a very wide and deep field, and you start developing a better understanding of the concepts as you get deeper into it. There are too many things that can only be understood with time. The practical application of some concepts is very important for bringing them into a habit.

For instance, many new traders don't pay attention to time decay while they are picking options contracts. It has a serious impact on the value of the contract. In the same way, implied volatility is a core area on which experienced traders focus specifically and make it a part of their core strategy, whereas new traders pay no attention to the concept of implied volatility. It is important to understand that all the numbers given on the chart hold some meaning, and it is important to take them into consideration. The option sellers have a lot more at stake, and that's why they engage professionals to calculate the premiums and do all the calculations. If you try to make a profit in options contracts without developing a thorough understanding of the concepts, you can get into serious trouble.

This is a reason new traders need to start from the beginner's level.

As a trader, you must also choose your broker wisely.

Popular Brokerage Firms

- Merrill Edge
- TD Ameritrade
- E-Trade
- TradeStation

There are several things that you must look into a broker.

Qualities to Look for in a Broker

- · Minimum Account Balance required
- · The fees and commissions
- · Options trade cost
- · Account fee and other charges like annual fees, closing, and inactivity fee
- · Tradable securities
- · Tradable securities provided
- · Mobile application if available
- · Kind of research of data provided by the brokerage firm
- · Customer support offered

Things to Look for in Your First Options Contract

The premium of an options contract is not much. It is usually a fraction of the actual cost. However, you must not forget that you can't buy options contracts as per your desired quantity. You can only buy options contracts in lots of 100.

Therefore, even if you are buying the options for XVZ company at a premium price of $5, your total cost of a lot would be $500.

Therefore, you must make the decision diligently. There are several important decisions that you must make.

They are:

- · Speculation of the trend in the desired stock
- · An assumption of the price that the stock that it can achieve
- · The time frame in which it can achieve the target price

Speculating the Trend

This is the most important decision that you must make. You will have to first determine whether the price of the stock would go up or down. This will help you in determining whether you should buy a call option or a put option.

Target Price Assumption

You will also have to determine the price that the stock can achieve before the expiration date. It is crucial that you select the target price, also called the strike price carefully. If you have bought a call option and the stock remains below the strike price, it will become out of the money, and you will not get anything at the time of expiration.

Call Options Contract

For instance, you pick the stock of XYZ company trading @ $50

The premium is $5

The expiry is one month ahead.

Your target price or the strike price would be above $55.

To remain profitable, the stock will have to go beyond $55. If it remains below that, then you will lose money.

Put Options Contract

The same rule applies to a Put Options Contract.

If the stock is currently trading at $50

The premium is $5

The expiry is in one month

The strike price would be anywhere below $45.

If the stock goes below $45, you will gain money.

If it stays above that price, you will lose money.

Chapter 13: Managing Options Positions

In options trading, the investor can take two different positions – a short or long position. The investor can sell an asset (going short) or buy it (going long).

Ordinarily, you will think that is all, but this position is further complicated by the two types of options – the put and call option.

What this means is that the investor can take four different positions – a short call, a short put, a long call, and a long put. Additionally, experienced investors can combine short and long positions to form complex trading and hedging strategies.

Long Position

During a long position, which is also a buy position, the investor is anticipating a rise in the price of the stock. Such a rise in the stock price will be profitable for the investor.

A long call position is a situation where the investor buys a call option. Therefore, a long call position is also beneficial if the price of the stock rises.

The basic concept behind the long aspect is the same as that of a long call. The value of a put option rises when the option or asset drops in value.

In terms of the long position profits, the potential loss in a long asset purchase is the purchase price of the option. However, the upside is limitless.

Moreover, for the long calls and puts, the profit downsides are complicated.

Short Positions

The second position in Options Trading is the short positions. It is the opposite of the long position explained. The investor anticipates a decrease in the price of the option to gain profit. Executing a short position is not as easy as when you buy an asset.

Using a short stock position as an example, the investor expects profit if the price of the stock drops. This is possible by borrowing a number of shares from a stakeholder of a particular company while selling it at the current price.

With this, the investor has an open position for the number of shares he or she bought with the broken. Remember, this stock has a particular timeframe before it will be closed.

Peradventure, the price of the stock drops, the investor has the right to buy the number of stock shares lower than the total price he sold them.

The excess cash for this trade is the profit of the investor.

Most investors find it hard to understand the idea behind short selling; however, it shouldn't be complicated. Well, to clarify this, the example below can make things clear for you. If, after this, you do not understand, then Options Trading is not for you.

Assuming the stock of NCE is currently sold for $50 per share. For some reason, you anticipate a fall in the price of the stock and decide to sell short in order to make gain from your anticipation. How then should your short sale look like?

- You place a margin deposit as collateral to your broker to give you a loan of 100 stock shares
- With the loaned shares given to you, you sell it at the price of $50 per share. With this, the share isn't yours anymore; however, in your account, you have $5,000

($50 x 100 = $5000). In this situation, you are short of stock because you are in debt of 100 shares to your broker.

- Assuming your expectation that the price would fall happens gradually. After some weeks, the price dropped to $30 per share. Furthermore, you expect the price not to go any lower, so you decide it's time to close the sale.
- You then bought the 100 shares at the price of $30, amounting to $3,000. You decide to repay the 100 shares of stock you borrowed from your broker.
- With the 100 stocks, you were able to make a profit of $2,000 by activating a short trade. When your broker loaned you the shares, you received $5,000 ($50 x 100 =$5000), and after buying, you were able to pay back your loan amounting to $3,000. Amount received ($5,000) – Amount Paid ($3,000) = Profit ($2,000)

Short positions are usually given to accredited investors because it requires a high level of trust between the broker and the investor in order to execute this deal. Actually, it doesn't matter if the short is executed; the investor must place collateral that the broker will use in exchange for the loan you want to take.

Other Short Positions

A short call position is activated when an investor sells a call option. The position is the opposite of the long call. The seller is in a better position to profit short call position is activated, and the value of the asset or stock drops.

Alternatively, when the investor triggers a put option, the seller profits if the value of the option traded is higher when compared to the predetermined option price.

Options trading come with varieties of long and short positions for you to adopt during trading. A knowledgeable investor who understands the advantages and disadvantages of all individual positions will always be ahead of the market.

However, if you are a new trader, don't rush to apply for these positions. Understand each position before making an effort to combine into your trading strategy.

Chapter 14:   Multiplying   Your Money Flow With Options Trading

There are a couple of things each investor should remember when exercising options trading. Let us teach you what these things are.

Movement of Market

The major focus of the inexperienced investors is on the falling and rising of underlying asset prices. But simply implementing strategies for generating profit from upside and downside movement of the market is just not enough as these strategies fail if the movement stops or becomes insignificant. Sometimes the market is not volatile, and the shift in the prices of the underlying stocks is so less it does not even matter. Call options are dependent on the rising of prices or generation of profits, while the out-of-the-money options lose all of the investments if there is no rise in the stock prices. Therefore it is really important to think about the strategies you are implementing and the state of the market before starting the trade. The market conditions may not always be as favorable in the short run as they are in the long run, and as a consequence of this, long-term options are costlier.

Stock Charts

A stock chart is a plotting of various attributes of the stocks on a chart; these attributes are majorly prices and the timeframe. It is important for an investor to read up on stock charts according to the options they're planning to buy. There are stock charts for different timeframes, such as one month, three months, or even the whole year. Reading the charts informs the investors about how the prices are moving in a market within a specified timeframe. The rise and fall of the stock prices can be easily noticed from these charts, and this information can be used to create a plan for the investment and options trading. It is not enough to see just the one-month chart as the prices in the chart may seem to be stable, but that may not really be the reality. Sometimes the movement in prices is quite slow and can only be actually noticed over a longer timeframe. From the recent changes in the prices of the underlying stock, an investor can speculate on the future movement of the prices. The speculation may not always be up to the mark as a few other factors can shake up the market unexpectedly.

Move with the Trends

An investor can determine the ongoing trends in the market by studying the stock charts. Usually, when a market is following a trend for a considerable amount of time, it is expected that it will continue to do so. Using this speculation, the investors try to make money off these trends. Going against the trends in some situations can be fruitful, but it is rare, and usually, betting against the trends causes the occurrence of losses. Trends are seldom interrupted in the short term, and it is not easy to beat them; therefore, a newcomer trader is suggested to move with the trends.

Limiting the Losses

Losing in the options trading market is nothing new. Everyone loses once a while, but what actually matters is how much you've lost and if there is a way to limit this loss. Assume a trader has a well thought out plan for earning big profits, but due to some reason, his plan fails and he is starting to lose. Now the ideal thing for the investor to do should be limiting the loss at the earliest. Losing a percentage of your total investment is still better than losing all of your investment; therefore, it is important for an investor to know when to pull back and sell their position to minimize the losses.

Option Chain

Option chains are a listing of all the call and put options that can be purchased for a given underlying stock. These different types of options are further separated in the list in different columns. Not only the types, but the strike prices and expiration dates of the options are also mentioned in this list. There is another attribute call volume of the contracts, which is a statistic of how often a specific control is traded. Repeatedly traded contracts have a higher volume, and the contracts that have never been traded or traded really rarely have volume zero. Investors are often suggested to go with the contracts having a higher volume as more trades indirectly points to more chances of success in their exercises. Similarly, options with higher strike prices and a long expiration period are recommended for the investors. Purchasing options with less volume of these attributes is full of risks and is not recommended for inexperienced traders. The market is also considered to be more volatile during the opening and closing hours of the day. The shift in the activity with the time of the day should also be noted by the traders.

Cash is King

The trading tip "Cash is king" is applicable in more than just one context, and that is why it's so valuable. It also builds upon our last tip about cutting your losses.

Basically, "cash is king" simply tells you to deal with any difficult situation by separating your emotions from it. Say, you're expecting a stock to move up, but it doesn't. It's reasonable to get anxious in this situation and have second thoughts about your plans. That's when you separate your emotions from the situation by taking the cash off the table.

How do you do this? You take half your money and cash it out by selling your position, leaving the other half on the table to give it more time. The biggest benefit of this is the peace of mind, which should certainly not be underestimated. At the end of the day, you will be much less stressed about your position and much more capable of enjoying a good night's sleep. And secondly, you will be protecting yourself against huge losses while also ensuring you don't completely miss out on big profits.

Chapter 15:   How to Become a Millionaire with Options Trading

There is more to options day trading to just having a style or a strategy. If that was all it took, then you could just adopt those that are proven to work and just stick with them. Yes, options day trading styles and strategy are important, but they are not the end-all-be-all of this career.

The winning factor is the options day trader himself or herself. *You* are the factor that determines whether or not you will win or lose in this career. Only taking the time to develop your expertise, seeking guidance when necessary, and being totally dedicated allows a person to move from a novice options day trader to an experienced one that is successful and hitting his or her target goals.

To develop into the options day trader you want to be, being disciplined is necessary. There are options day trading rules that can help you develop that necessary discipline. You will make mistakes. Every beginner in any niche does and even experienced options day traders are human and thus, have bad days too.

Knowing common mistakes helps you avoid many of these mistakes and takes away much of the guesswork. Having rules to abide by helps you avoid these mistakes as well.

Below, I have listed 11 rules that every option day trader must know. Following them is entirely up to you, but know that they are proven to help beginner options day trader turn into winning options day traders.

Have Realistic Expectations

It is sad to say that many people who enter the options trading industry are doing so to make a quick buck. Options trading is not a get-rich-quick scheme. It is a reputable career that has made many people rich, but that is only because these people have put in the time, effort, study, and dedication to learning the craft and mastering it. Mastery does not happen overnight, and beginner options day traders need to be prepared for that learning curve and to have the fortitude to stick with day trading options even when it becomes tough.

Losses are also part of the game. No trading style or strategy will guarantee gains all the time. In fact, the best options traders have a winning percentage of about 80% and a losing average of approximately 20%. That is why an options day trader needs to be a good money manager and a good risk manager. Be prepared for eventual losses and be prepared to minimize those losses.

Start Small to Grow a Big Portfolio

Caution is the name of the game when you just get started with day trading options. Remember that you are still learning options trading and developing an understanding of the financial market. Do not jump the gun even if you are eager. After you have practiced paper trading, start with smaller options positions, and steadily grow your standing as you get a lay of the options day trading land. This strategy allows you to keep your losses to a minimum and to develop a systematic way of entering positions.

Know Your Limits

You may be tempted to trade as much as possible to develop a winning monthly average, but that strategy will have the opposite effect and land you with a losing average. Remember that every options trader needs careful consideration before that contract is set up. Never overtrade and tie up your investment fund.

Be Mentally, Physically and Emotionally Prepared Every Day

This is a mentally, physically, and emotionally tasking career, and you need to be able to meet the demands of this career. That means keeping your body, mind, and heart in good health at all times. Ensure that you schedule time for self-care every day. That can be as simple as taking the time to read for recreation to having elaborate self-care routine carved out in the evenings.

Not keeping your mind, heart, and head in optimum health means that they are more likely to fail you. Signs that you need to buckle up and care for yourself more diligently include being constantly tired, being short-tempered, feeling preoccupied, and being easily distracted.

To ensure you perform your best every day, here a few tasks that you need to perform:

- Get the recommended amount of sleep daily. This is between 7 and 9 hours for an adult.
- Practice a balanced diet. The brain and body need adequate nutrition to work their best. Include fruits, complex carbs, and veggies in this diet and reduce the consumption of processed foods.

- Eat breakfast lunch and dinner every day. Fuel your mind and body with the main meals. Eating a healthy breakfast is especially important because it helps set the tone for the rest of the day.
- Exercise regularly. Being inactive increases your risk of developing chronic diseases like heart disease, certain cancers, and other terrible health consequences. Adding just a few minutes of exercise to your daily routine not only reduces those risks but also allows your brain to function better, which is a huge advantage for an options day trader.
- Drink alcohol in moderation or not at all.
- Stop smoking.
- Reduce stress contributors in your environment.

Analyze Your Daily Performance

To determine if the options day trading style and strategies that you have adopted are working for you, you need to track your performance. At the most basic, this needs to be done on a daily basis by virtue of the fact that you are trading options daily. This will allow you to notice patterns in your profit and loss. This can lead to you determining the why and how of these gains and losses. These determinations lead to fine tuning your daily processes for maximum returns.

Pay Attention to Volatility

Volatility speaks to how likely a price change will occur over a specific amount of time on the financial market. Volatility can work for an options day trader or against the options day trader.

It all depends on what the options day trader is trying to accomplish and what his or her current position is.

There are many external factors that affect volatility, and such factors include the economic climate, global events, and news reports. Strangles and straddles strategies are great for use in volatile markets.

There are different types of volatility, and they include:

- Price volatility, which describes how the price of an asset increases or decreases based on the supply and demand of that asset.
- Historical volatility, which is a measure of how an asset has performed over the last 12 months.
- Implied volatility, which is a measure of how an asset will perform in the future.

Be Flexible

Many options day traders find it difficult to try trading styles and strategies that they are not familiar with. While the saying of, "Do not fix it if it is not broken," is quite true, you will never become more effective and efficient in this career if you do not step out of your comfort zone at least once in a while. Yes, stick with want work but allow room for the consideration that there may be better alternatives.

Conclusion

At every level of options trading, there are mistakes that people do over and over again. However, these mistakes must be avoided in order to realize a profit from the trade.

If you ever hope to make money in trading options successfully, then there are a number of skills that you are going to want to hone as much as possible, starting with the ability to trade like a robot. When you have a trade on the line that could make or break you it is only natural to be scared or anxious, but those emotions are only going to cloud your judgment if left unchecked which is why it so important to box them up and bury them in the ground when you are trading so you can only focus on the facts in front of you. Fail to do so, and you will watch in fear as your sure thing turns into a huge loss as opposed to jumping into action right away in order to salvage as much profit as possible.

Being a successful trader means being able to react at a moment's notice, without hesitation, full stop. The only way you can ever ensure that this is going to be the case is if you can put aside the emotional aspect of what is occurring and focus on the numbers as if it was some else's money. A good way to ensure that this is possible is to make it a point of never putting more on the line then you can afford to lose.

The first emotion you are going to need to learn to banish is anger, as it can cloud your judgment without you even realizing it. It is perfectly natural to feel angry when a trade that was going your way suddenly ends up costing you money, that doesn't mean that it is ever the right choice to act on that anger as no good will come of it whatever you might believe at the moment.

While doing what the major players in the market do can be a reliable strategy, following the crowd at all times is not advisable in the long-term. Successful traders do their own research and trust themselves enough to act on the results they determine, even if they mean making trades that might seem unpopular at the moment. When it comes to seeking substantial payouts trading against the market is going to be the most likely, if not the most reliable, option. This is only the case if you do so for the right reasons, however, as being contrarian just for the fun of it isn't going to get you any either.

Most of the market movement that takes place each day is caused by sheep who simply follow the crowd with no real idea as to why they are doing what they are doing. Successful traders don't fall into this mindset; however, instead of being a sheep, you should strive to be a wolf, which means improving your intuition through a combination of practice and diligent study. Eventually, all this hard work will pay off, and you will start to become more confident in yourself, which will then make it even easier to trust in yourself, and not the sheep, moving forward.

It is natural to feel a tinge of fear when you get a signal that your trades are down or if the market as a whole is experiencing a dramatic upheaval. If you don't control this instinct, however, then it can be easy to overreact and find yourself getting rid of your holdings or turtling up and not taking any risks until the perceived crisis has passed. While this will likely lead to fewer losses, it will also negatively affect the potential for additional gains.

In order to bypass this natural reaction, it is important to be aware of what fear really is, which is simply a natural reaction to stimuli that can be perceived as a threat. If you find yourself becoming afraid during stressful stock-related scenarios, you may find it helpful put the situation into a larger context or to take a moment to consider what it is that you are really afraid of. Either of these exercises will allow you to put the fear on hold and think rationally about the situation, which will make it much easier to ignore entirely.